To my mother, Gerri, for her endless love

JANETTA OTTER-BARRY BOOKS

Text and photographs copyright © Suzi Eszterhas 2014

The right of Suzi Eszterhas to be identified as the author and photographer of this work has
been asserted by her in accordance with the Copyright, Designs and Patents Act, 1988 (United
Kingdom).

First published in Great Britain and in the USA in 2014 by
Frances Lincoln Children's Books
First published in paperback in Great Britain in 2015 by
Frances Lincoln Children's Books,
74-77 White Lion Street, London N1 9PF
www.franceslincoln.com

A catalogue record for this book is available from the British Library.

ISBN 978-1-84780-656-7

Printed in China

135798642

tiger

SUZI ESZTERHAS

Frances Lincoln
Children's Books

After a long night of hunting
in the forests of India, a mother tigress
carefully returns to her den. She crawls
into this secret place where she has
hidden treasure – her tiny babies.
The babies are called cubs and she is
the only one in the whole world
who knows they are there.

The three tiny cubs are striped from head to tail. At only three weeks old, the cubs are very wobbly on their paws, but they are curious about the world outside their den. Sometimes, when Mum is off hunting, they sneak outside and take a peek.

The tigress and her cubs are happiest when they are tucked away inside their den. The tiger den is a cave on a rocky cliff. This home is cool and protects the family from India's hot summer sun. Hidden and snuggled up against their mother's enormous body, the cubs are also safe from danger that is lurking in the forest.

The young cubs are hungry, and Mum makes milk inside her body for them to drink. Mum's milk tastes yummy and is full of special vitamins that will help the babies grow, and develop strong muscles and bones. The cubs grow slowly. It will take two years for them to grow into their stripes.

One day the mother tigress decides it's time to move to a new place. She takes the cubs on a forest walk to find a good spot to call home. This is the first time the little cubs have ever walked in the open. Being away from the den is scary, but also exciting. The cubs are careful to follow the steps of Mum's giant paws and they stick to her side like glue.

In their new den, the family rests in the open. The leaves on the ground are like a blanket, and the tigers pile on top of each other in a heap of stripes. Like every tiger on earth, each of the cubs has its own different stripe pattern. It is just like a human fingerprint.

Mum doesn't have much time to rest. After a quick 'cat-nap', she is awake and busy caring for her family. She licks her cubs to keep them clean and also to keep them cool in the heat. Mum's biggest job is to protect the cubs and she will growl fiercely at any sign of danger. The cubs learn from watching her, and soon they are practising hissing.

The little cubs have a lot to learn, and they start by playing. The rock wall of the den is smooth like a slide, and the cubs go up and down, over and over again. Mum is also fun to play with – they pounce and tumble on her soft, furry body, and even chew on her tail. This is all good fun, but it is also a way for the cubs to build muscle and learn how to move their bodies.

After six months, it's time to go on adventures with Mum and explore their world. A tiger's world is called a territory. Mum's territory is big and full of new, exciting places to explore and the cubs are eager to see everything. They climb rocky hillsides, crawl into dark caves, cross grassy meadows and stroll through thick forests.

Soon the cubs are big enough to follow their mother on hunts and watch how she catches food. Mum uses her powerful eyes and strong sense of smell to find deer from very far away. Her striped body helps her blend into the grass and disappear, so she can slowly creep up on the deer. She moves very slowly so as not to make a sound, and will freeze like a statue if the deer look her way.

The cubs practise their own hunting skills. They like to pounce on sticks and other forest toys. Their catch is just a stick for now, but it helps prepare them for hunting real deer.

When the cubs are a year old, they still love to play. They even have boxing matches. It may look like fighting, but they don't hurt each other. This kind of play prepares the cubs for life as grown-up tigers and helps them be alert and fast, so they can escape danger and defend themselves – just like their mother.

Water is a huge part of the tiger family's life.
They need to drink every day to stay healthy.
In the summer the tigers spend hours soaking
in water to stay cool. Waterholes are like
a tiger's swimming pool, and the cubs have
a great time splashing and jumping.

At the end of two years, the cubs are spending their last days with their mother. They are fully grown and are now the largest cats in the world. They have become great hunters. Their stripes, and the skills they have learned from their mum, have allowed them to blend into the forest and become almost invisible to deer.

The young tigers are now ready for the biggest adventure of their lives. They must each go out to find their own space. Thanks to their mother's never-ending care, they are strong and healthy, and know how to stay safe. One day very soon, they will rule a territory of their own.

More about Tigers

- Tigers live on the continent of Asia in grasslands, forests and swamps.

- Tigers are the largest cats in the world. Male tigers can weigh up to 317 kilograms or 700 pounds, and are up to 3.35 metres or 11 feet long.

- Tigers have incredible eyesight and can see six times better than a human.

- Tigers have stripes on their skin as well as on their fur. If you shaved off the fur of a tiger, the striped pattern would remain the same.

- Tigers have very rough tongues. This helps them rid their prey of fur and feathers, with a few firm licks.

- A tiger's roar is very loud and can be heard up to three kilometres or two miles away.

- Tigers retract their claws when walking. They do not leave claw marks in their footprints.

- In addition to deer, tigers also hunt sloth bears, wild dogs, leopards, crocodiles and pythons, as well as monkeys and hares.

- Tigers can live to be 15 years old in the wild.

- Tigers are endangered because people hunt them for their fur and body parts. There are less than 3,200 wild tigers in the world.

- For more information visit http://www.tigertime.info

COLLECT ALL THE BOOKS IN THE EYE ON THE WILD SERIES –
A BRILLIANT INTRODUCTION TO ANIMALS IN THE WILD, FROM BIRTH TO ADULTHOOD

Elephant
978-1-84780-655-0

Follow an elephant calf from his birth on the African grasslands to adulthood, photographed
close-up in the wild by award-winning photographer Suzi Eszterhas. See the calf learning to use
his trunks and tusks, playing in the waterholes and meeting other young elephants.
At last, when he is fifteen years old, the elephant is ready to leave the herd
and explore the African plains by himself.

Cheetah
978-1-84780-307-8

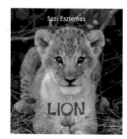

Lion
978-1-84780-311-5

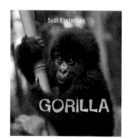

Gorilla
978-1-84780-305-4

Orang-utan
978-1-84780-313-9

Brown Bear
978-1-84780-308-5

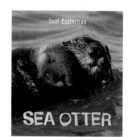

Sea Otter
978-1-84780-203-3

"Stunning photos make this a series which will appeal to all animal lovers"
– *Parents in Touch*

Frances Lincoln titles are available from all good bookshops.
You can also buy books and find out more about your favourite titles,
authors and illustrators on our website: www.franceslincoln.com